This is one of a series of books on modern art created to help very young people learn the basic vocabulary used by artists, a sort of ABC of art. Parents and teachers play a key role in this learning process, encouraging careful, thoughtful looking. The book isolates storytelling aspects of works of art to show how they are used by artists and how they contribute to meaning in art. By looking for stories and discussing what ideas and feelings they suggest, adults encourage children to develop creative thinking skills. At the back of this book, there is more information about the pictures to help in this engaging process.

Enjoy looking together!

Stories

Philip Yenawine

Stories

The Museum of Modern Art, New York

Permissions and copyright notices:
Page 4: © 2006 C. Herscovici, Brussels/Artists Rights Society (ARS), New York
Page 5: © 2006 Salvador Dali, Gala-Salvador Dali Foundtion/Artists Rights Society (ARS), New York
Pages 6, 11, 13, 19: © 2006 Artists Rights Society (ARS), New York/ADAGP, Paris
Page 7: Reproduced by permission of the Henry Moore Foundation
Page 8: © Estate of Dorothea Lange
Page 9: © Succession Miró/Artists Rights Society (ARS), New York/ADAGP, Paris
Page 14: © Lichtenstein Foundation
Page 16: © 2006 Artists Rights Society (ARS), New York
Page 17: © 2006 Succession H. Matisse, Paris/Artists Rights Society (ARS), New York

Second edition 2006

Library of Congress Control Number: 2006924453
ISBN: 978-0-87070-178-8

Published by The Museum of Modern Art
11 West 53 Street
New York, New York 10019
(www.moma.org)

Distributed in the United States and Canada by D.A.P., Distributed Art Publishers, Inc., New York

Distributed outside the United States and Canada by Thames & Hudson Ltd., London

Front cover: Detail of Marc Chagall, *Birthday*. 1918.
Oil on cardboard, 31 $^3/_4$ x 39 $^1/_4$" (80.6 x 99.7 cm).
Acquired through the Lillie P. Bliss Bequest

Back cover: Detail of René Magritte, *The Empire of Light, II*. 1950.
Oil on canvas, 31 x 39" (78.8 x 99.1 cm).
Gift of D. and J. de Menil

Printed in China

In pictures, you can make up stories about people...and places...and things.

Details (clockwise from upper left): Marc Chagall. *Birthday* (p. 19); Henri Matisse. *The Piano Lesson* (p. 17); Salvador Dali. *The Persistence of Memory* (p. 5); Andrew Wyeth, *Christina's World* (p. 15)

Sometimes the stories are a little like whispering secrets.

Paul Gauguin. *The Moon and the Earth*

And they can be mysterious.

Odilon Redon. *Silence*

They can play tricks. Is it daytime in this picture, or is it night?

René Magritte. *The Empire of Light, II*

Can you tell the time on these pocket watches? What else is strange about this picture?

Salvador Dalí. *The Persistence of Memory*

Maybe it's time to eat. What meal is this? How can you tell?

Pierre Bonnard. *Dining Room Overlooking the Garden (The Breakfast Room)*

Some paintings and sculptures show families being together.
What can you tell about this family?

Henry Moore. *Family Group*

Can you tell more about these parents and children? Pretend you know them.

Marisol (Marisol Escobar). *The Family;* Dorothea Lange. *First Born, Berkeley*

You have to use your imagination to figure out who is the mother, father, and child in this family.

Joan Miró. Plate V [The Family] from *Series I*

You can also make pictures of the city — full of buildings, cars, and signs. Look at the colors and lines. Can you hear any noise?

Jean Dubuffet. *Business Prospers*

Here's an old-fashioned movie theater. What do you think the young woman is thinking?

Edward Hopper. *New York Movie*

How is this man feeling? What do you think he is looking at?

Marc Chagall. *Self-Portrait with Grimace*

How many differences can you find between this woman...

Roy Lichtenstein. *Girl with Ball*

and this one? Make up a story about what they are doing. How do you think they feel?

Andrew Wyeth. *Christina's World*

What are these three girls doing?
Where do you think they are?

Jacob Lawrence. *In the North the Negro had better educational facilities*

Do you think this boy wants to practice the piano? Where do you think he would like to be instead?

Henri Matisse. *The Piano Lesson*

These girls are swinging from a pole.
Does it seem dangerous?
What about the building behind them?

Ben Shahn. *Liberation*

Look at these two people. Where are they? What are they doing?

Marc Chagall, *Birthday*

Pictures are almost like dreams.
Here is someone sleeping on a patchwork quilt.
Does she look comfortable?

Romare Bearden. *Patchwork Quilt*

Maybe she is dreaming of a quiet night and a gentle lion. What else can you imagine about this story?

Henri Rousseau. *The Sleeping Gypsy*

Do you have any secrets or mysteries to draw? Any funny stories to tell in pictures?

The art in this book can be found at The Museum of Modern Art in New York City. Other museums and galleries have many interesting pictures too, and it is good to make a habit of visiting them, looking for stories. You can also look in magazines, books, buildings, parks, and gardens.

Page 2
Paul Gauguin
The Moon and the Earth. 1893
Oil on burlap
45 x 24 ¹/₂" (114.3 x 62.2 cm)
Lillie P. Bliss Collection

Finding in Tahiti an essence he felt missing in his native France, Gauguin often drew the local people and terrain of his adopted home, creating his own myths and archetypes.

Page 3
Odilon Redon
Silence. c. 1911
Oil on prepared paper
21 ¹/₂ x 21 ¹/₄" (54.6 x 54 cm)
Lillie P. Bliss Collection

Trying to probe essential mysteries, Redon often created cryptic scenes such as this, representing silence with a symbolic gesture, downcast eyes, deep shadows, and spiraling lines.

Page 4
René Magritte
The Empire of Light, II. 1950
Oil on canvas
31 x 39" (78.8 x 99.1 cm)
Gift of D. and J. de Menil

Magritte's form of Surrealism (going beyond what we perceive to be real) involved depicting recognizable phenomena in impossible relationships.

Page 5
Salvador Dalí
The Persistence of Memory. 1931
Oil on canvas
9 ¹/₂ x 13" (24.1 x 33 cm)
Given anonymously

Dalí, another Surrealist, went further in imagination than Magritte, incorporating real and distorted elements to create disjointed, dreamlike images.

Page 6
Pierre Bonnard
Dining Room Overlooking the Garden (The Breakfast Room). 1930–31
Oil on canvas
62 ⁷/₈ x 44 ⁷/₈" (159.6 x 113.8 cm)
Given anonymously

Bonnard's work depicts domesticity through beautiful colors, warm light, and sketchy brushwork that seems to be forever fresh, if slightly distorted.

Page 7
Henry Moore
Family Group. 1948–49 (cast 1950)
Bronze
59 ¹/₄ x 46 ¹/₂ x 29 ⁷/₈"
(150.5 x 118 x 75.9 cm)
A. Conger Goodyear Fund

In Moore's sculpture a pattern of interlocking forms and rhythmic contours help symbolize family unity and harmony.

Page 8
Marisol (Marisol Escobar)
The Family. 1962
Painted wood and other materials
in three sections
Overall 6' 10 ⁵/₈" x 65 ¹/₂" x 15 ¹/₂"
(209.8 x 166.3 x 39.3 cm)
Advisory Committee Fund

Marisol's fatherless group has the spare,
straightforward simplicity of Depression-
era photographs, a family perhaps impov-
erished but not poor.

Page 8
Dorothea Lange
First Born, Berkeley. 1952
Gelatin silver print
19 ¹³/₁₆ x 15 ¹³/₁₆" (50.4 x 40.2 cm)
Purchase

Direct and honest, Lange used no artifice
to picture the unsentimental but still ten-
der bond between a father and infant.

Page 9
Joan Miró
Plate V [The Family] from *Series I*. 1952
Etching, engraving, and aquatint,
printed in color
Plate: 14 ¹⁵/₁₆ x 17 ⁷/₈" (38 x 45.4 cm);
sheet: 19 ³/₄ x 26" (50.2 x 66 cm)
Curt Valentin Bequest

Miró often adopted methods that seem
childlike in his attempt to cut through
acquired knowledge to more basic under-
standings of things.

Page 11
Jean Dubuffet
Business Prospers. 1961
Oil on canvas
65" x 7'2 ⁵/₈" (165.1 x 220 cm)
Mrs. Simon Guggenheim Fund

Both intrigued and put off by the force of
modern life, Dubuffet employed a very
edgy line and strong colors in his cartoon-
like, slightly macabre representations of
people and places.

Page 12
Edward Hopper
New York Movie.1939
Oil on canvas
32 ¹/₄ x 40 ¹/₈" (81.9 x 101.9 cm)
Given anonymously

Hopper's paintings employ rich colors
that seem to glow with light and also
clearly evoke a mood full of associations
and memories.

Page 13
Marc Chagall
Self-Portrait with Grimace. c. 1924–25
Etching and aquatint, printed in black
Plate: 14 ¹¹/₁₆ x 10 ³/₄" (37.3 x 27.4 cm);
sheet: 20 ⁷/₈ x 15 ³/₈" (53.0 x 39.1 cm)
Gift of the artist

Appealingly unglamorous, Chagall pres-
ents himself as a wide-eyed energetic
man, his character enhanced by the distorted mouth.

Page 14
Roy Lichtenstein
Girl with Ball. 1961
Oil and synthetic polymer paint on canvas
60 ¹/₄ x 36 ¹/₄" (153 x 91.9 cm)
Gift of Philip Johnson

Both amused and inspired by cartoon
imagery, Lichtenstein capitalizes on styl-
ized and stereotypic simplifications that
become signs and emblems, rather than
accurate descriptions of arms, waves,
and tossed hair.

Page 15
Andrew Wyeth
Christina's World. 1948
Tempera on gessoed panel
32 ¹/₄ x 47 ³/₄" (81.9 x 121.3 cm)
Purchase

This woman's back is turned to us. We
are unable to see her expression, yet eas-
ily able to picture ourselves in her place.
Our empathy perhaps explains the paint-
ing's enormous appeal.

Page 16
Jacob Lawrence
In the North the Negro had better educational facilities. 1940–41
Tempera on gesso on composition board
12 x 18" (30.5 x 45.7 cm)
Gift of Mrs. David M. Levy

Lawrence painted a visual history of African Americans, documenting their experience in moving North to search for greater opportunity, including better schools.

Page 17
Henri Matisse
The Piano Lesson. 1916
Oil on canvas
8' 1/2" x 6' 11 3/4" (245.1 x 212.7 cm)
Mrs. Simon Guggenheim Fund

Wedged into Matisse's studied gray composition is a slice of green, the shape of which is mirrored in the boy's face—perhaps an indicator that the boy's mind might be outside, away from the ghostlike visage behind who seems to monitor his practice.

Page 18
Ben Shahn
Liberation. 1945
Tempera on cardboard, mounted on composition board
29 3/4 x 40" (75.6 x 101.4 cm)
James Thrall Soby Bequest

Deeply engaged with social issues and history, Shahn here drew children intently playing above the rubble of a war-torn city, perhaps a symbol that, despite all, the spirit is indomitable.

Page 19
Marc Chagall
Birthday. 1915
Oil on cardboard
31 3/4 x 39 1/4" (80.6 x 99.7 cm)
Acquired through the Lillie P. Bliss Bequest

Influenced by Surrealism, Chagall combines autobiographical references and other aspects of reality with elements of fantasy in order to create a metaphor for feelings, such as pleasure at the first awareness of pregnancy.

Page 20
Romare Bearden
Patchwork Quilt. 1970
Cut-and-pasted cloth and paper with synthetic paint on composition board
35 3/4 x 47 7/8" (90.9 x 121.6 cm)
Blanchette Hooker Rockefeller Fund

This stiff figure at rest on Bearden's *Patchwork Quilt* resembles an ancient statue, rigid but timeless and regal, and represents a mix of folk and ancient art in a modern image.

Page 21
Henri Rousseau
The Sleeping Gypsy. 1897
Oil on canvas
51" x 6' 7" (129.5 x 200.7 cm)
Gift of Mrs. Simon Guggenheim

Rousseau was untrained in artistic technique but uninhibited in creating large imaginary tableaux, mysterious because of their flights of fancy.